Lisa Bellear (1961–2006) was a Goenpul woman of the Noonuccal people of Minjerribah, Queensland. She was a respected poet, photographer, activist, spokeswoman, dramatist, comedian and broadcaster. Her work in social justice, campaigning for equality and Indigenous rights, and her contribution to Indigenous writing, academia and the arts had a huge impact on many Aboriginal and Torres Strait Islander communities. Notably, Lisa was a presenter on Melbourne's 3CR radio network's *Not Another Koori Show*, and performed her poetry in Australia, North America and across Europe. *Dreaming in the Urban Areas* was her first, and only, published poetry collection.

T0307558

First Nations Classics

DREAMING IN THE URBAN AREAS

LISA BELLEAR

First published 1996 by University of Queensland Press
PO Box 6042, St Lucia, Queensland 4067 Australia
Reprinted 2007
This First Nations Classics edition published 2024

University of Queensland Press (UQP) acknowledges the Traditional Owners
and their custodianship of the lands on which UQP operates. We pay our
respects to their Ancestors and their descendants, who continue cultural and
spiritual connections to Country. We recognise their valuable contributions
to Australian and global society.

uqp.com.au
reception@uqp.com.au

Cover design by Jenna Lee
Typeset in 11.5/16pt Bembo Std by Post Pre-press Group, Brisbane
Printed in Australia by McPherson's Printing Group

  First Nations Classics are assisted by
the Australian Government through
Creative Australia, its principal arts
investment and advisory body.

Australian Government

Creative
Australia

This project is supported by the Copyright Agency's Cultural Fund.

C©PYRIGHTAGENCY
CULTURAL FUND

A catalogue record for this book is available from the National Library of Australia.

ISBN 978 0 7022 6852 6 (pbk)
ISBN 978 0 7022 6989 9 (epdf)

University of Queensland Press uses papers that are natural, renewable and
recyclable products made from wood grown in well-managed forests and other
controlled sources. The logging and manufacturing processes conform to the
environmental regulations of the country of origin.

MIX
Paper | Supporting
responsible forestry
FSC
www.fsc.org   FSC® C001695

A Family Tribute to Lisa Bellear

Lisa Marie Bellear was of the Noonuccal people of Minjerribah who hail from the far north coast of New South Wales and Queensland. She was born in Melbourne on 2 May 1961 and adopted into a white family after the death of her mother. Growing up was a mixture of emotional trauma and sadness; both from childhood abuse and not knowing who she really was, although she was sure she was not 'Polynesian' as the adoption agencies had put on her papers.

She discovered her natural family in her early twenties and began an amazing journey pursuing social justice for women and for her people. She also obtained two masters degrees (Critical/Historical Study from the University of Melbourne and an MA in Creative Writing from the University of Queensland) and was working towards her thesis for her doctorate. Sadly Lisa passed away in July 2006, leaving many people grieving and a mass of unfinished and unpublished work – these works will now only be read in the Dreamtime.

Lisa was passionate about social justice, photography, the St Kilda AFL Club and her poetry. She performed her poetry widely and was published in many journals and anthologies. The royalties from this new edition of *Dreaming in the Urban Areas* will go to a variety of Aboriginal charities. Everyone who was touched by Lisa will agree that this earth was left a better place for her having walked on it.

Contents

PART II – WHITE MAN APPROVAL

INTRODUCTION
by Kirli Saunders

I was born when Lisa Bellear, our beloved Noonuccal sis from Minjerribah, was writing this collection, which means I was blessed to be raised in a world that knew her words and was made better by them. *Dreaming in the Urban Areas* is as relevant and necessary now as it was when it was first penned in 1996.

Lisa Marie Bellear was born in Melbourne on 2 May 1961. After the death of her mother, Lisa was displaced and adopted into a white family with papers that identified her as 'Polynesian'. In her early twenties Lisa found her biological family and became passionate about pursuing social justice. In July 2006, while Lisa was writing her thesis for her doctorate, she sadly passed over into the Dreaming.

I didn't have the pleasure of meeting Lisa but, through her work and the rich accounts of respected blak academics, writers and friends, I know her to be an Aunty, Sis and family; one we'd call staunch and loving, with fire from the Old People shining through her and lighting the way. I'm told she was funny and raw, sensual and enraged, intelligent and honest. *Dreaming in the Urban Areas* was her first collection, and after her passing her family donated her royalties to the Judge Bob Bellear Diabetes Clinic at the Aboriginal Medical Service in Redfern.

Lisa Bellear was a human rights activist who spent fourteen years championing social and political change for her community at the University of Melbourne. She was actively involved in Koori communities in Victoria, especially with the Yuroke Students Aboriginal Corporation, Aboriginal Advancement League and Victorian Aboriginal Legal Service. Lisa's poetry brings to light her experiences of governance and bureaucracy, inherent racism, false doctrines, and the systematic oppression of our people then (and now).

In *Dreaming in the Urban Areas*, Bellear's words themselves are unassuming, colloquial and gutsy. She claps back with the language of the oppressor and speaks with conversational sarcasm:

I mean how could I, a white middle-class woman,
who is deciding how can I budget when my man won't
pay the school fees and the diner's card club simply
won't extend credit.
I don't even know if I'm capable
of understanding
Aborigines, in Victoria?
Aboriginal women, here, I've never seen one …

She takes the personal and makes it universal, offering her poems as salve for her loved ones, for the Mob, and for the activists and poets we adore like Tony Birch and Gary Foley. This collection is a blak time capsule transcending past, present and future. It honours the humanity and survival of First Nations Peoples in the current – post-referendum, pre-treaty – local and broader global political context where First Nations Lands are being brutally occupied just as they were at the time of her writing. *Dreaming in the Urban Areas* unpacks connection to and caring for Country, paying homage to the Traditional Owners, while examining Lisa's contemporary experiences as a First Nations person in Naarm:

There are maybe two red river gums
a scarred tree which overlooks the
Melbourne Cricket Ground the
survivors of genocide watch
and camp out, live, breathe in various
parks 'round Fitzroy and down
town

> *cosmopolitan*
> *St Kilda*

And some of us mob have graduated
from Koori Kollij, Preston TAFE,
the Melbin Yewni

Red river gums replaced
by plane trees from England
and still

      the survivors
            watch.

There's also a current of hope woven throughout this collection – a sassy, blak, joyful resistance underpinning the dream of a different future – one that can only be imagined with the truth being told. With warrior-woman directness, she holds to account the prime minister, the institutions and systems – colony, patriarchy and white feminism:

Eh Professor, big shot,
Big cheese, or whoever
You claim to be
You've really no idea
Love to chat sister,
But there's faxes to send
And protest letters to write

Lisa honours refusal and paves for us a decolonial, matriarchal, blak sovereign path. In turn, her Ancestors directly address Lisa encouraging her to continue to fight, to dream, to rest by the fire for a moment:

and through the
flames, the embers

and the burnt chops
and charcoaled
potatoes wrapped in foil
they're saying, tidda girl
you're okay,
keep on dreaming
keep on believing

Now she's one with the Dreaming and through these poems Lisa Bellear, as Ancestor, speaks to us. She offers us earthy rhythm and meditative confrontation, with warning and welcome to go slow, to understand and to keep fighting for change.

PART I

COME DANCIN'

Grief

This is not about love or
hurt or hate

This is not about
battery hens, McDonald's hamburgers

This is not about
acid rain or conspiracy theories

This is about me
my life, my grief my
need to maintain
the capacity to love.

July 1994

Hanover Street Brunswick 3056

on a bright sunny afternoon

Cruisin' – on my way with a keen
sense of purpose: milk (full cream),
toasting bread, cigarettes, papers
... a woman's day

Sensor rays connect with a thirty
centimetre 'white' child who sits
joyously on a three-wheeled
plastic bike

I feel safe enough to share
my smile

As we check each other over
with carefree knowing smiles –
his parents raise their heads
through the pruned rose bush

In twenty years time will
he remember this warrior woman –
I wonder

September 1995

Writer's Block

To warm my hands
I boil the kettle,
two teaspoons
of ideologically unsound
coffee go lovingly
into a medium size
porcelain mug
half a dessertspoon of
made in Australia honey
dash of carnation milk.

I remove my gloves
grasp the mug
with both hands
and tell myself
blue sky, sunshine
and central heating.

My hands warmed
I begin to
write.

July 1993

Women's Liberation

Talk to me about the feminist movement,
the gubba middle-class
hetero sexual revolution
way back in the seventies
when men wore tweed jackets with
leather elbows, and the women, well
I don't remember or maybe I just don't care
or can't relate.
Now what were those white women on about?
What type of neurosis was fashionable back then?
So maybe I was only a school kid; and kids, like women,
have got one thing that joins their schemata,
like we're not worth listening to,
and who wants to liberate women and children
what will happen in an egalitarian society
if the women and the kids start becoming complacent
in that they believe they should have rights
and economic independence,
and what would these middle-class kids and white women do
with liberation, with freedom, with choices of
do I stay with my man, do I fall in love with other
white middle-class women, and it wouldn't matter if
my new woman had kids or maybe even kids and dogs
Yes I'm for the women's movement
I want to be free and wear dunlop tennis shoes.
And indigenous women, well surely, the liberation
of white women includes all women regardless …

It doesn't, well that's not for me to deal with
I mean how could I, a white middle-class woman,
who is deciding how can I budget when my man won't
pay the school fees and the diner's card club simply
won't extend credit.
I don't even know if I'm capable
of understanding
Aborigines, in Victoria?
Aboriginal women, here, I've never seen one,
and if I did, what would I say,
damned if I'm going to feel guilty, for wanting something
better for me, for women in general, not just white
middle-class volvo driving, part time women's studies
students
Maybe I didn't think, maybe I thought women in general
meant, Aboriginal women, the Koori women in Victoria
Should I apologise
should I feel guilty
Maybe the solution is to sponsor
a child through world vision.
Yes that's probably best,
I feel like I could cope with that.
Look, I'd like to do something for our Aborigines
but I haven't even met one,
and if I did I would say
all this business about land rights, maybe I'm a bit
scared, what's it mean, that some day I'll wake up
and there will be this flag, what is it, you know
red, black and that yellow circle, staked out front

and then what, Okay I'm sorry, I feel guilt
is that what I should be shouting
from the top of the rialto building
The women's movement saved me
maybe the 90s will be different.
I'm not sure what I mean, but I know that although
it's not just a women's liberation that will free us
it's a beginning

September 1991

Chops 'n' Things
for Eva Johnson

I can't wait to curl around
a lemon scented tree
light a fire and
watch it burn down to
the embers as the sun
floats away, far away
our ancestors are
yarning and laughing
at this Koori woman
and through the
flames, the embers
and the burnt chops
and charcoaled
potatoes wrapped in foil
they're saying, tidda girl
you're okay,
keep on dreaming
keep on believing

September 1991

9

Historical Journals
for Tony Birch

Historical journals offer frameworks
to
        rationalise
        demistify
and
        historisise
constructs of deception
Reference points
are
        neutral
        safe
settler • explorer • coloniser • drovers • dyke

Reach for truth

June 1994

To the Palawa

Bbrrr can you feel change
snow again in Palawa
country

Hmm I think, I wonder
are they the only blackfellas
left alive who lived
in the snow country

Mt Bulla
Mt Bogong
Mt Kosciusko
Mt Hotham
And Mt Donna Buang

What happened
to our Koori Brothers / Sisters
whose land is
Snow Country

What happened?

July 1995

Woman of the Dreaming

My sweet woman of the Dreaming
Where is your soul,
I need to surround your body
With my spirit, the spirit
Of the embodiment of love
>anger
>pain
>disparate neutrality

My sister, lover, friend
Let your soul and my soul
Fall in love

But love is so remote
The gum trees are whispering
The Yarra Yarra is polluted
Koalas on Phillip Island are
So stressed that they too will
Be another victim of the
Invasion

1990, the beginning of the
Haul towards the new country
Where do you fit in my sister
No one but you know you
No one but me know the love
I have for the world but ...

More apt the love I have
For you

    Sweet
    Strong
    Determined
    Misunderstood
Woman of the dreaming
Find you soul,
And peace and love and
Eternal fire and spirit will
Connect with our ancestors
And our land
Will begin to smile, again.

September 1990

Feelings

Like Douwe Edberts
Freeze dry coffee
I stand motionless
But full of feelings
Gin, native, abo, coon
An inquisitive academic
Then asks, 'Are you Aboriginal?'

Do I punch
Do I scream
Do I raise my arms
To ward off
The venomous hatred
Which institutionalised
Racism leaves unchallenged
As they collect their evidence
To reinforce their 'superiority',
And our 'inferiority'

Am I Aboriginal
Am I Torres Strait Islander
Am I South Sea Islander

I laugh inside, at her ignorance
I shake my head,
But how can I pity
A person who is identified

As the expert exponent on
Indigenous Australians

Eh Professor, big shot,
Big cheese, or whoever
You claim to be
You've really no idea
Love to chat sister,
But there's faxes to send
And protest letters to write

I turn and walk away
Preserving my dignity
Without humiliating hers.

October 1992

Urbanised Reeboks

In a creek bed at Baroota
I lose myself amongst
the spirit of life of
times where people
that is Blak folk
our mob – sang and laughed
and danced – paint-em
up big, red orchre
was precious ... go on
remember-hear the
sounds of flattened
ground and broken gum
leaves –

My feet slip out of their
urbanised Reeboks
of sadness, which
hides its loneliness
behind broken Reebans*

Uncloaked feet hit
the earth ...
And its okay
to cry

September 1993

* I coined this word 'reeban' – it comes from combining the words
'Reebok' and 'Ray-Ban'. I love wearing these types of shoes and
sunglasses.

Fashion Statement

Rayboks and reebans
And jeans with holes
And photographic chemicals
That leave a pattern
Of blotched bleached
Benign dreams

Henna your hair
If you dare
The smell
Of leather

Give out energy
Strong powerful
Black women's energy

Look at those
Wudjella women
Wanting a piece of
My womanist energy

Fantastising fanatically
On how we are women,
Are oppressed and in
Our oppression we are
United

Thanks tidda girl –
My wudjella sister
For your thoughts
And love and whatever

But I'm in love
With my Koori community
I'm in love
With Black women

Henna your hair
If you dare ...

October 1990

Afraid to Love

Dry rot ached through her heart
Can't love, don't need
Anyone, not even you.
Curse your beauty,
Curse your art.
Encumbered by love
She cries.
Alone.

June 1993

Just Send a Fax

I'm not alone
or lonely
neither sad
nor miserable,
just a bit
homesick
and sometimes missing
people, who I
may occasionally
take for granted.

June 1993

Just for Tonight

for Damita Brown

I'll wish on the moon
Full of thanks
For realisation / of dreams
I'll lean her photo
Against my ghetto-blaster
Love / in love / yeah
Just for tonight

February 1992

Regrets

Passion crept silently through
the vase of red roses, releasing
unmet, unspoken thoughts
of overwhelming lust,
make her move, quick, now
stricken by Catholicism, she
sits paralysed and gazes
nonchalantly and in a
rotarian public speaking voice,
asks off-handedly, 'More tea
Sarah?'

June 1993

Leave a Message

Yesterday I needed
To talk,
Leave a message
After the beep, however
If you wish to send
A fax, kindly press
The asterisk button
On your phone, after
This message has ended:
'Now that you've bothered
to call, don't waste that
thirty cents'
'Nobody home at the
moment …'
'I answer correspondence
in the morning'
I've got a name
For being a listener
Yeah, but even listeners
Need to
Talk.

June 1993

The Beginning?
for Toni Lawson

Three weeks have passed
and tomorrow
Three weeks and one
day will have passed
since we – you and I
held hands
sweet isn't it
falling down across
backwards sidewards
totally totally totally
in love

June 1995

Come Dancin'

I want to dance with
something tangible, other
than my shadow
Let's you and me
cascade across the
lounge room floor

I shift the couch
you pour the wine
Let's then dream
I can be happy
You can laugh

The lounge room
becomes a paradise
where pain and undiagnosed
nervous conditions
desist

July 1993

Pursued

There is a phone call
I shake my head persuasively
no! Communicating through
congested hand movements
no – no – no – not home!

Sharp glares from a sister
who denies by existence
oh, I think there's a community
meeting, or perhaps a rotary club
dinner – you understand?

Reacting to interrogation
resisting personal discussion
she exclaims exasperated
look! I'm not
my sister's keeper

July 1993

The Dream

Yes, I have a dream
Yes, I have a dream

And yes, yes, yes
if I don't-want-it-like-it-is
I'm gunna keep our
warrior ancestor spirits
alive Yes, Yes, Yes,
if that dream is revealed
to be wrong-safe-immoral
then I'm gunna fight for
change 'til I fly high
with our warrior ancestor
spirits

September 1995

Mr Prime Minister (of Australia)

Dear Mr Keating,

Hi there, it snowed today, up in the Blue Mountains. I'll
never complain about Melbourne weather again. Good luck
with 'Mabo', actually Mr Keating, you will need the spirit
and energy from a 100, 000 year history.

Unfortunately Australia is immature. Even the talk of
'Republicanism' is rather immature while there is continual
denial that this country is Aboriginal Land.

I'll be honest with you, I am frightened, racism is a disease;
do you ever wonder what manifests from diseases that
haven't received adequate treatment, say for over 200 years.

As Prime Minister, a leader, you have an enormous but not
Impossible task, of moving 'Australia' forward, to becoming a
republic.

If you need support, like to talk.

Yours Sincerely,

A. Citizen
(Noonuccal)

June 1993
Varuna, Katoomba

Beautiful Yuroke Red River Gum

for the Northlands Secondary College Mobile Rebel School

Sometimes the red river gums rustled
in the beginning of colonisation when
Wurundjeri,
Bunnerong,
Wathauring
and other Kulin nations
sang and danced
             and
                  laughed
                     aloud

Not too long and there are
fewer red river gums, the
Yarra Yarra tribe's blood becomes
the river's rich red clay

There are maybe two red river gums
a scarred tree which overlooks the
Melbourne Cricket Ground the
survivors of genocide watch
and camp out, live, breathe in various
parks 'round Fitzroy and down
town
           cosmopolitan
              St Kilda

And some of us mob have graduated
from Koori Kollij, Preston TAFE,
the Melbin Yewni

Red river gums replaced
by plane trees from England
and still
           the survivors
              watch.

                                        September 1994

Mr Don't Scratch My Rolex

Him, that fulla over there,
        from the Lands Council
       he doesn't care
how us women feel,
   about mining,
     we milk our children
       our tomorrow
on breasts filled with poisons
comes from that sludge
     in the river
'member how we could walk into
       mmm the clearest sweet
               water
and the
    barramundi,
    all
        gone,
true, him that fulla up there!
I seen his
   mobile phone
     toyota dreaming,
       nothin' but first class
           travel,
where to now,
Canberra?
New York City?
I'd love to see them mob

32

                              at Geneva,
                              the ILO,
                              I'd tell 'em
                              our story,
                              women's business,
and show 'em this is not our
                              way,
Aboriginal country
                    is seeping
                    in misery,
                    death.

I weep for our dreaming
          hold
                me
                    sister
                    I
                              need
Your strength,
got to keep believing
          that
          somewhere
             someone
                    cares.

                                        June 1993

The Sounds of Little Children

Oh I hear the sounds of
little children, *I wunt, gimme*
gimme, wah wah, he-she
took my lollies

Smack Wack Go
play nintendo an'
stop all that sookin'
report to yer mother

One minute goes by
and one more and one more
in a reflective and introspective
pre-menopausal mood, I begin
to want for the nuances of
little children to echo and dance through
the quiet crisp country
air

April 1995

34

A Friendly Soul

A vacancy sign appears
on the lower left hand side
of the window on the first floor:
another 'roomy' 'inmate' 'friend' 'lover'
has gone, passed away, is visiting
the Dreamtime.

There is a service
four are in attendance, including
the minister and the owner of
the boarding house.

Yes, she nodded reverently
Mavis was an exemplary boarder:
she never smoked in bed and was
always on time with her payments.

I'll miss her gaiety, her smiling eyes:
Mavis, was a special woman and
my friend.

June 1993

Mother-in-Law

Took me thirty years before I left your father
Battered wife syndrome, well that's the term the
Social worker used at the neighbourhood centre
Oh I didn't realise I was being abused. On the bad days
I never left the house, told friends, not that I had many
I was visiting a relative who had taken poorly
Look at me sweetheart, you've made the right decision
Believe me, you have to think of Stacy, and don't forget
You have to take care of yourself. Mothers have rights
Mothers have needs too. I'll not make excuses for
Your behaviour. You have to work through that, nor
Can you say it was all Larry's fault. Honey don't cry
Together we'll be okay, you've got to stop hating yourself
Alright, the court order allows fortnightly access visits
On the proviso he's not been drinking – listen he's not
Doing right by you or Stacy, coming here drunk. He
Hasn't even bothered to shave. Darling, he may still care
He may even still love, but rules are there for the protection
Of the child, and for the sanity of the mother. Maybe the
Next time you will be able to welcome Larry inside but
For now, tonight, the situation, the reality is no, and if
He's still there in five minutes, Larry knows the score
There's a train, or there's a police van
It's up to him

June 1993

36

Spiritual Ruin

Glass houses are easily broken
by hypocritical leaders
whose ethics are as disposable
as babies' nappies
Believe me, for the good of
the country, you'll thank me
in the long run!

I cannot stand to watch
glass houses shatter
with insincerity and mendicity

Yet, even I cannot cast a brick
nor shoot an AK-47 and be able
to justify my destruction.

In my room, with a two bar heater,
I fall quietly into a world
of perennial perdition.

To yell, to throw anger
is wasted. I seek comfort
by snuggling up to my pillow,
and lying still under the doona
covers
the electric blanket
on high.

June 1993

A Peaceable Existence

I dream / I dream / I dream
of a world
a beautiful
world
that exists
above the clouds

There is
love
there is hope
there is
peace / equality
and social justice

There is
no need
for signs
proclaiming
Land Rights

There is
no need
for anti-
discrimination
legislation

Let me
fly above
the clouds

Let me
breathe

July 1993

Survivin'

for Susan Duffy

Shadows dancing around my soul
Good girl, bad girl
Very very sad
Too damn loud
Oh so happy
Off with its head
Slice its tongue
Deny its vision
Crush the spirit
Reaching for stars
That exploded eons away
Dancing without
Romance,
Alone / by myself
And still able
To love,
I am survivin'

June 1993

To Wilfred Tapau

Sardines circle Mer
entangled by bala Wilfred
boilem up good now
sitting down on Zomred land
rice n' damper
fresh coconut juice
mmm straight from the
tree to our island table
table cloth an' all
ocean breeze Islander gospel
music, thank you bala Wilfred
and the spirits of Mer

June 1994

PART II

WHITE MAN
APPROVAL

Artist Unknown

*for all Indigenous/colonised artists inspired by a visit to the Art
Gallery of New South Wales to look at Destiny Deacon's work*

Artist unknown
Location Liverpool River
The Rainbow Serpent
Narama and her sons 1948
Acc p1 1956

Artist unknown
Kimberley Area
Hammerhead Shark
And Black Fish 1948
Acc no p15 1956

Artist unknown
Location Oenpelli
Mimi Family 1948
Ochre on cardboard
Original collection presented by
The Commonwealth Government
Acc no p116 1956

Artist unknown
Location
Ochre on cardboard
Mimi man and woman 1948
Acc no14 1956

Artist unknown
Location Milinginbi
Hive of wild honey 1948
Ochre on cardboard
Acc p24 1956

Artist unknown
Location Oenpelli
Crocodile
Ochre on cardboard
Acc no p17 1956

Artist unknown
Location Oenpelli
Two fish 1948
Acc p19 1956

Artist unknown
Divisions of fish
Acc no 22 1956

Artist unknown
Ochre on cardboard
Acquisition number
And purchase date
No name
No tribe
Or clan
Or Language group

No gender
No spirituality
The unknown artist
reads like a memorial

December 1993

Souled Out

Only $200 – Ladies /
Gents and you could
Become an Aborigine
For two whole days!
Hey lady, what's sar matter
Haven't you seen
One before?
Come and experience
The lifestyles and
Mystical spirituality
That is quintessential
To the life and existence
Of a Traditional Aborigine
We'll also have a real
Properly initiated Elder
Who will empower you
With Dreamtime secrets
From an ancient culture
And for an extra fifty bucks
We'll throw in some
Real live witchetty grubs
And eat them, just like
The Natives did all those
Dreamtimes ago.

June 1993

Bureaucrats' Battleground

Yes you can!
No you can't!
Next please.

Excuse me
are you sure
you filled in the form
correctly?

Ha, you forgot to sign –
include incorporation papers,
Sorry, can't process
until all the requirements are
met, wouldn't be fair
to the other applicants

Under Regulation 6.1.5 F
your organisation is eligible
for a community enterprise
initiative grant,
however if you require funding for
capital equipment and administration
you'll have to make another appointment
fill out different forms.

Can't you read? Want to
see the manager – I am
the manager. This office closes
at 4.30, call back Monday.
If we didn't stick to union rules,
we'd never get home.

I'm sorry if you missed the deadline
may I suggest you work at
being more organised, there
are some training packages that
would help, but not right now
read the sign!

He focuses hard on the bath
his partner will have ready –
rose oil, glass of champagne
a Havana cigar.
He'll pat the dog, and kiss
the children, and she'll ask how
was his day, at the
bureaucrats' battleground.

June 1993

White Man Approval

Tidda girl you talkin' me!
Eh white man approval
And all that shit

Universities and bureaucrats
ATSIC officers
And CDEPs and EEOs
And Ab Study grants

Forms, fuckin' forms, fuckin' forms

Submissions, deadlines, and whyte boards,
And computers that spell
And draw columns and pretty pictures
That calculate what project
Some long-socked akubra hat-tanned gubbah
Says fits the procedural manual
Within the confines and constraints
Of self-determination
Of self-management
Of economic independence

Your hair's too curly
Your nose doesn't go splat
Freckles, blue green eyes
Urbanised

Your spirit is black
White man's approval?
Nah tidda girl not me
But eh ... what about ... what about ...

September 1991

Christmas in Cuba
for Chrystos

To assess the revolution
Our revolutionary friends
Visit Cuba at Christmas
Nicaragua in Novemeber
Algeria in April
And Timor on Tuesdays

If it weren't for millionaire
Socialists imagine how ignorant
Australia would be

And relevance to
Indigenous Australians
All this blood and genocide
Throw in apartheid
Shake vigorously
Chief Buthelezi, Mandela and De Klerk

What have we?
A litany of lies
Which tells the world
Including South Africa
We don't have an 'Aboriginal Problem'
Australia's lucky
Australia's white

Life and someone else's revolution
In countries I can't spell and pronounce
Fade quickly, as the jungars★
Kick my head between
Two telephone books
And SCREAM
'Fuckin' Abo … you want rights'

★ police

January 1992

Travels on a Train: 1

Hey, you don't mind if I drink?
Got a couple of spares – no!
Would you have a cigarette … and a light?
Sure you don't want a charge – eh,
Oh your missus would kill you?
Well what about me, left the Kings Tavern
In Sydney, round 5.00 am, caught a train
Stopped in Penrith, then on to Katoomba
Wanted to see me little girl, and me
Mother-in-law wouldn't let me in the house,
Here, have this, cost me $48.00, na go on,
Brought up me wife's favourite VSOP.
Damn, so, I'd had a few drinks, big deal.
She just stood there, blocking the steps, between
Me, my little girl, and me ex missus. Look, for awhile
I gave up the grog, for two months and one week,
Even found steady work on a building site, that
New complex, well I come home one day and there
Was my missus, getting down with another bloke.
I followed that court order, work and don't drink
And that's what happens, used to bring me pay packet
Home unopened, true! And I ask what's left for me?
She goes running home, takes the kid, end of story.
Sure you don't want the brandy …
Thanks for the cigarette.

June 1993

Mostar

for Stan Kvesic

They are bombing
the town, the town, the town
where my father
was born

He is Croatian,
they are Muslim
he is Serbian
they are Muslim
he is Bosnian
they are Muslim
they could be
our sister
our aunt
our cousin

When the bombing
stops, when
quite air spills out
coagulated blood
we can come home

Victory
Glory
Triumph
Accolades

And UN Peace Negotiators
And Red Cross unemployed truck drivers
From Australia, 3000 a month
Eighteen hour days, not bad

When the deal is photographed
When Reuters, AAP, confirm peace
We can go home
That's how it's supposed to go
But I don't feel right.

August 1993

Breathalyser

Pull over now, the
fluorescent blue light
yells, firmly but politely
Blow into this bag
and may I see
your licence?

Remain calm there
are no smells or
traces of illegal activity
within my car
which has a
land rights sticker
on the back window

And yet somehow
I feel guilty!

June 1993

Ode to Nelson Mandela

Why Mr President does your
ANC dominated government
which is conveniently based
on a patriarchal model
why Mr President do you
allow-sanction-not
question the continual
sale of arms to
the former Rwanda government
Why Mr President Why

Can you share with
me / us all colonised
peoples, all colonised
nations and 'oppressive'
'brutal' 'alien' 'coloniser
countries' just one
justification for your
government's sale of arms
to the Former members of
Rwandan government who
are now currently in Zaire
regrouping, reassessing the
Stage II plan

G for Genocide

... Mr President?

June 1995

Mmm Tastes Divine

So Hugh Grant is sorry, huh sorry,
sorry-sorry-for what. That he
Mr so fucking cool got caught with
something up and something down?
That he's sorry sorry so fucking sorry
for being sprung, sprung bad, man,
with Miss *Mmm* Divine Brown
who is African-American.
Huh Hugh, what are You sorry for
Your white girlfriend
Your white heritage
Your white values; middleclassness.
And whatever will the Oxford Alumni
think?

Mr so fucking cool dreamy eyed
Hugh Grant: so you done it / at / with
a beautiful blak woman with beautiful
luscious lips; don't go round being
sorry, ashamed, just be honest and
next time – brother 'cos you know the
score – don't bother apologising for
finding blak, women of colour, sexy and
desirable.

June 1995

Hate Fuelled with Kerosene

Embalmed by hate
Undisciplined urges
As soon as the
Jerry can is
Fuelled with kerosene
They wait for darkness

She and her partner
Are ready, they have
The courage of two
750 mil bottles of bourbon
And a doctorate in colonisation.

Anxiousness becomes usurped
By euphoria, we'll burn that
Bora ring, we'll axe that
Scar tree, there won't be
Any more Aboriginal rights
Meetings in that Community
Centre, ha, not after tonight.

They begin to fight
Over who should take
Credit, for lighting the first
Match, quickly he
Rabbit punches his girlfriend
Not too hard, but calculated

Enough, so he can
Be the hero,
Down at the local
Golf Club,
They'll buy him bourbon
Shout him beers
Then in the cover
Of self-righteousness
He and his taken
For granted assistant
Will fuel their hate
With more kerosene
And perhaps this time
Just for a laugh
They'll borrow two
Twelve gauge double
Barrelled shot guns.

June 1993

Awake Our Warriors

for Gary Foley – A warrior

Seven stages of grief
seven generations of unrecoverable recovery
The hurt
The anger
The lies – deceit

Wounded dangerously
Our warriors awake
through the smog filled haze
of colonisation

There will be justice
There must be justice
NOW!

September 1995

Inevitability

A black brother dies alone
A black sister weeps aloud
There was a vision
There were dreams
And then came colonisation

A black child is removed
from her black family
and their black families white /
black / friends and 'lations

For their best / own interests
black child cries alone
black child weeps inside

A white adoptive mother / father /
brother / sister ignore the young
cries   pain   grief

Black child dies   alone
And still we
are removed ...

September 1995

The Rapist

That man is
a rapist
I cannot forget

Rape is rape
is rape is rape

And yet the
sickness and anger
that exists within
when I see
this rapist

He is a man
respectable collar and tie
and men's pants job
This particular
rapist targets
Black women
This rapist is
Black white people
call him Mr
His 'lations
call him Uncle /
Grandpa / cuz / bud

I call him
a rapist!

July 1993

Pissing in Parks
for Destiny

It's 6.30 am or 5.35 pm
The dog and the dog owners
Are pissing in parks
And I'm dodging the shit
And the piss and the
Glass and the needles
And I photograph a blade
Of Grass, the solitary
Piece that has not
Begat doggie do
And I'm planning to write
To local council
in protest of curfews imposed
On kids in the streets after dark

Give me gangs and teenage wankers
And old people who
Unearth the flower beds
To brighten their uneventful lives
In an uneventful culture
That doesn't give a fuck
About their elders

Eh give me teenage Ninja turtles
And gummies that spit and yell abuse
At the casual passerby

But dogs and their owners
Who piss in parks, who
Kill the grass ...

I've sent that letter to council

November 1990

Tanna Man
for Faith Bandler

Cuts cane
As white men
With long slim noses
And whips
Curse him,
Faster 'nigger' harder.

Each piece of can he cuts
represents an islander from home,
kidnapped, black birded, stolen.

Mango trees echo vision
Freedom, isn't meant to be
a luxury for idle white boss men
to contemplate and dwell.

June 1993

Colonisation

Our lands littered,
our dead
our pain
our sorrow
our hearts awash
with grief

no new moon
can ever replace
never replace

August 1994

Freedom Mandela

Nelson Mandela
Nelson Mandela
One man, one freedom
United Black Nation
27 years of mindless oppression
He be free now.
Open up the kruggerand,
Open up the South African Airways

Freedom, freedom
Thank you Mr Hawke on congratulations freedom
Thank you Mr Hawke for enacting ATSIC
Thank you Mr Hawke for Ab Study grants.
For reintroducing tertiary fees
For enabling Kooris, Gooris, Nungas, Murries, Wongais
An opportunity to learn the white man's way
And yet retain our culture
Thank you for self-determination
Thank you for self-management
For police raids, and other callous calculated bashings
Of five of my brothers ...
Can I make a phone call *bash*
I'm entitled to ... *bash*

Freedom. Can one man represent so much
No gripes about our Koori Nation
No big deal that non-Koori Australians can rejoice over

Freedom Mandela
But if you can think
Remember your own backyard
Is where it really counts.

February 1990

The Promise

I'm gonna learn
to drive a car,
a big flash red one,
with government number plates,
before I die.

I'll deliberately slow
down past bus and tram stops
look out for brothers and
sisters and friends
who must resort weekly
to wheeling shopping trolleys
to their local supermarkets.

I know, I recall:
wind, rain, heat, pollution
still, the family has to eat
and I remember, all too well
the brothers, the sisters who
sped past tram stops
in their big flash red cars
with gubbament number plates
how cumbersome; the shopping
trolleys, they didn't have time

to stop, their sardonic
laughter was crueler
than any Melbourne
winter.

June 1993

A Rural Tragedy

for Tracey Moffatt

Grab the axe
begin to swing
there is light in
her eyes
she curses the sun
three months of rain
three months of drought
thirty years
of a husband
who cursed her harder
than any plague of locusts

She blinks and swings
he falls and calls
no stop, you're mad
you crazy bitch

Just say the word
and you'll be saved

Hmm he loves that
prize heifer more
than me

Three seconds
time is up

No word of love
no tender thoughts
damn the sun
she lifts the axe
and begins to swing
again, and again, and again
and again and again and again
and again and again and again
and again and again and again
and again and again and again
and again ...

July 1993

77

The Smoker

Blair came at me with
flashy white teeth
impeccably groomed
blue black hair that
lay captured by a
Tiwi design pure silk scarf.

Babe, how that word
oozed vociferously through
the damp bed sitter which
was home

Babe, do you mind if
I smoke, the brand
was the same as my
father's: unfiltered camel

I open the nearest window
and comment banally on
the weather. That
seemed like a safe
enough topic.

June 1993

Pushed

Pushed! pushed! constantly
he tried, God how he tried
and tried, and tried and tried
to die

Maybe his totem, his
dreaming, his Aunty
kept tellin' him stay
stay, stay
stay alive
survive

We'll never know
I wonder if
he will.

June 1993

Baby Basher

Daddy can't cope
with his daughter's
fears
six weeks old, such
incredible lung power

He grabs Bonnie's legs
and throws her
against the bedroom
wall

The crying stops

Relieved, Daddy turns on
the sports channel and
pours himself a
cold one

July 1993

Break the Cycle

Hit
me
again
and
i
swear
i'll
call
the
cops /
brother
got
to
stop
fightin'
me
i'm
your
sister

June 1993

Taxi
for Joan Kirner

splashed by a passing cab,
and another and another
there's rules you see;
don't. stop. for.
black women, accelerate
past black men
and pensioners on pension day
can't trust,
trash
got no cash
we're all *nuisances*
reminders of an unjust
world, where the poor
people of colour
are at the mercy
of even taxi drivers.

June 1993

Justice?

Adopted, fostered,
Sexually abused
Colonised, Christianised
booris buried brutally
by settlers, in sand,
kicked their heads, off,
but who cares for Kooris
who mourns for Murries
and as I walk
on Wiradjuri land
'discovered' by Lawson
I sense that I am angry
Treaty, Compact, Reconciliation
Mabo, 1788, Land Rights, Sovereignty
Bicentennial Celebrations,
The Royal Commission into Aboriginal
Deaths in Custody, 339 Recommendations
The deaths don't stop,
The mourning; the grieving is
there, all around, for 205 years
There is
no justice.

June 1993

White/Blak Professor
for Vicki-Anne Speechley-Golden

The cruelty of their dismissal
is immeasurable – cannot hear
will not hear
Tears are swept along the
channel sewers
white / blak all the same
when no one listens, no
Respect

Talk n' Talk n' may be
some tribal dance, the
White / Blak University
Professor nods and half
smiles

shadows–alienation–a
humourless death

No more talk
No more tribal dance
No more
No more
No more

You see But you don't!
You hear But you won't!

I will dream for now
But your spirit cannot
will not ever rest

There is no room now
For tears
There is no space, now
For forgiveness
sadness-sickness-death
White / Blak Professors'
You had your
chance ...

You had your
chance ...

You had your
chance ...

Shame
On
You!

June 1995

A Suitcase Full of Mould

Imagine alienation
Imagine a bonding process of
23 years of lies,
Of 23 years of guilt
Of being estranged
Of trying to let go …
Of wanting to but …

Imagine being 12
Of being home and sick
And have someone who you trust
Or someone who you think you trust …
Imagine not being able to tell,
Of wanting to
But you have no one to tell

Hey where are all the social workers.
When you need them,
Or when you think you do.

Imagine being 13,
Coming home from boarding school
To care for a person
Called mum who has once again collapsed
Too much booze,
Too much mental torture
Too much, too much, too much

Try being 14 and look out
Your lounge room window,
It's dark now but someone who you love
Or someone who you think you love
Is gardening
Imagine gardening at 9 pm
What is her fascination
With the gladiolas, the daffodils,
Those beautiful blue, pink and purple petunias

Oh that's right there's beer cans
Strategically placed in different
Sections of our beautiful beautifully
Manicured flower beds.

They say flowers grow for beauty
No, not for me
Flowers grow to hide
The inability to cope
Too much, too much, too much

Forget forget forget
As much as I try
I cannot, there must be
Some reason, some reason
Why so many, so many
Kooris, Noongahs, Murries, Nungas,
Go through
The nightmare

Why, why, why
I don't know why
All is know is here I am at 23, 24 at
26, 36 and 46
If I live that long
I'm wondering, searching, questioning
I don't know why
Should it matter, I'm one
Of the lucky ones

A suitcase full of mould
Contains those few precious memories
Of my years, without my people
The photos
The children's books
A painting of a lighthouse I drew at 12
Short sharp memories
A collection of
My life which,
If I could have a child
If I wanted to, I would
Give to them

Hey tell us about
Your life growing up ...

A suitcase full of mould
Is my childhood
A suitcase full of mould
A suitcase full of mould.

April 1989

Acknowledgements

Poems from this collection have previously appeared in the following publications: *Australian Multicultural Book Review, Australian Women's Book Review, Hecate,* 'Indigenous Women Community Education Conference Report', *Journal of the Australian and New Zealand Student Services Association, Koori Times, Ngariaty Kooris Talkin, Out Loud, Perseverance Poets Collection, Refractory Girl, Southerly* and *Varuna.*

Several poems from this collection have previously been published in the following anthologies: *Australia for Women* (edited by Susan Hawthorne and Renate Klein, Spinifex Press, 1994); *Australian Short Stories* (edited by Bruce Pascoe and Lyn Harwood, Pascoe Publishing, 1994); *Australien Der Frauen* (Frauenoffensive, 1994); *Second Degree Tampering* (Sybylla Press, 1992); and *Weddings & Wives* (edited by Dale Spender, Penguin, 1994).

The author would like to thank Arts Victoria for the writer's grant and Varuna Writers Centre for the fellowship that helped create the time and space for many of these poems to be created. The author would also like to thank the Victorian Writers Centre for its support.

Destiny Deacon, artist born of Kuku and Erub/Mer peoples, kindly gave permission for the title of her work, *Dreaming in the urban areas*, to be used as the title of this book.

FIRST NATIONS CLASSICS

Heat and Light by Ellen van Neerven
Introduction by Alison Whittaker

In this award-winning work of fiction, Ellen van Neerven leads readers on a journey that is mythical, mystical and still achingly real.

Over three parts, van Neerven takes traditional storytelling and gives it a unique, contemporary twist. In 'Heat', we meet several generations of the Kresinger family and the legacy left by the mysterious Pearl. In 'Water', a futuristic world is imagined and the fate of a people threatened. In 'Light', familial ties are challenged and characters are caught between a desire for freedom and a sense of belonging.

Heat and Light is an intriguing collection that heralded the arrival of a major new talent in Australian writing.

'A breathtaking work of art.' *The Weekend Australian*

'A stunning debut from a young writer of immense potential.' **Melissa Lucashenko**

ISBN 978 0 7022 6599 0

FIRST NATIONS CLASSICS

Purple Threads by Jeanine Leane
Introduction by Evelyn Araluen

Growing up in the shifting landscape of Gundagai with her Nan and Aunties, Sunny spends her days playing on the hills near their farmhouse and her nights dozing by the fire, listening to the big women yarn about life over endless cups of tea.

It is a life of freedom, protection and love. But as Sunny grows she must face the challenge of being seen as different, and of having a mother whose visits are as unpredictable as the rain.

Based on Jeanine Leane's own childhood, these funny, endearing and thought-provoking stories offer a snapshot of a unique Australian upbringing.

'*Purple Threads* reminds the reader that knowing the past helps us to understand the present and shape the future, and that interconnectedness is the human experience.'
The Weekend Australian

ISBN 978 0 7022 6602 7